Become a Coach

# Raving Fans of Become a Coach

*"This book gives a clear track to run on in becoming an excellent coach and advisor to others."*

- **Brian Tracy, Author, *The Psychology of the Sale***

*"Justin Lukasavige is a master! I've closely watched him grow his business over the years from nothing into an organization that's hitting on all cylinders. The time's long overdue for him to show YOU how to succeed and be profitable as a coach."*

- **Chuck Bowen, President of Chuck Bowen Coaching and host of *"The Chuck Bowen Show"* in San Antonio, TX**

*"In a day and age when it seems everyone wants to be a coach, Justin Lukasavige breaks down the formula necessary to turn your passion of helping others into serious profits. With "Become a Coach", Justin hits a home run. This should be required reading for anyone thinking about entering the coaching field. "*

- **Jay Peroni, CFP, President & CEO of Values First Advisors, founder of faithbasedinvestor.com, and author of *The Faith-Based Millionaire* and *The Faith-Based Investor*.**

Become a Coach

# And from People Just Like You

*"It's about time this book was written. It's a long overdue insiders guide to what it takes to succeed as a coach. If you want to live your dream of becoming a coach read this book before making the same mistakes that routinely force other coaches out of the marketplace."*

**- Rick Caron, Business Relationship Coach, thechiefconnector.com**

*"Become a Coach is a necessity for anyone wanting to use their gifts to help others. Don't make the mistake of thinking you'll be a great coach from the very beginning without first studying the industry and learning firsthand what it takes from one of America's foremost experts."*

**- Kent Julian, president of Live It Forward LLC (liveitforward.com) and founder of speakitforward. com. America's most sought after experts on intentional living, leadership, and REAL™ Success**

4

*"Your instruction manual on how to be successful, profitable and most importantly, a servant to others in a world where most people are takers."*

> **- Pierce Marrs, Sales Coach and President of Marrs Coaching, marrscoaching.com**

*"If you are considering becoming a personal coach, Become a Coach is a must read. Clear, fast paced and practical, Justin answers the pertinent questions with insight and generously shares resources to help you create a sound start."*

> **- Debbie Wilson, Lighthouse Ministries, Cary, NC, lighthouseministriesnc.org**

*"If you have made the decision to become a coach, or are just looking at possibilities, the next step is to get your hands on this book. "Become a Coach", is an easy read, concise and inspirational."*

> **- Joel Boggess, founder of 4pointscoaching.com, is committed to helping people find purpose and calling in the workplace.**

Become a Coach

*"Justin spills the beans on one of the fastest growing businesses without getting caught up in the hype of unrealistic expectations. This book is required reading before you become a coach."*

**- Jay Carter, Professional ADHD and Personal Productivity Coach, hyperfocusedcoaching. com**

*"Justin is the real deal. If you're considering a career in coaching this book is a must read."*

**- Jon Dale, Marketing Strategist, jondale.com**

6

# Become a Coach

## Discover What it Takes to
## Turn Your Passions into Profits

**Justin Lukasavige**

Become a Coach

Past Due: Press
527 Keisler Drive, Suite 204,
Cary, NC 27518
PastDuePress.com

To purchase more copies or to enquire about Justin visit www.lukascoaching.com.

ISBN: 978-0-9825465-0-5

Cover design and illustration by Nathan Fisher, ideasablaze.com
Editorial assistance provide by Alane Pearce, alanepearcepws.com

Become a Coach: Discover what it Takes to Turn Your Passions into Profits / Justin Lukasavige

ISBN: 978-0-9825465-0-5
1. Business  2. Education

Printed in the United States of America by PastDuePress.com

8

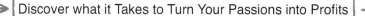 

To all those who have coached me over the years and helped make Lukas Coaching a success. Many have come along side me as coaches, mentors, consultants, pastors and friends. We've brainstormed well into the night to improve each other and our businesses. I, along with those I have coached, thank you.

Also, to my wife, Christine, who has been my biggest cheerleader through it all. There is no way I'd be living my calling right now if it weren't for you.

# Contents

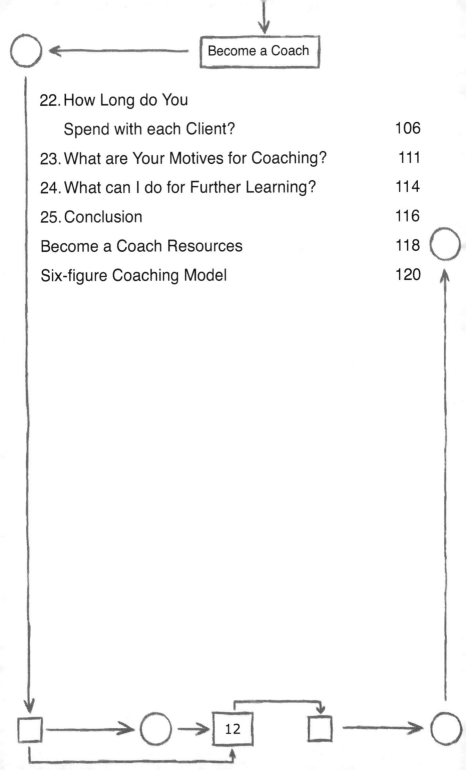

Become a Coach

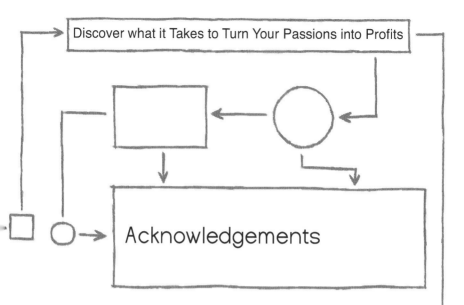

Discover what it Takes to Turn Your Passions into Profits

# Acknowledgements

A heartfelt thank you to my wife Christine for understanding that together we could provide a better life for our family. You have put up with me working into the night on many occasions. You understood when I worked two jobs simultaneously for nearly two years. You sacrificed at home with newborn children all while putting up with me building a business. Your will to maintain our lives through this transition has been a huge motivation to me.

To our children Ava, Amanda and Brie; many times I wanted to give in and work a little less. You remind me why I do what I do and you have a way of keeping me from

becoming too serious at times. I made the transition from a job where I traveled the majority of the time (which I did not enjoy) to a vocation in which I am blessed to live my passion every day. You three are the reason.

My sister, Rachel Lukasavige, provided many valuable insights for this book and helps me understand that focusing on my clients is the number one priority of my business. Without your valuable editing skills, I fear our readers would be forever lost.

Author and Coach, Dan Miller, and his wife, Joanne, have been great friends and mentors in many areas of over the past few years. I owe the success of my marriage to both of you and you continue to set the bar high. Christine and I humbly follow in your footsteps

I owe Dave Ramsey a large thank you for allowing my team and me to mirror the success of our business after yours. You showed me the ropes very early on in the radio studio and I'm forever grateful.

God is the ultimate architect. He knew what was in store for me before this idea was even a thought in my mind. While I never know what lies around the corner, I rest confident in the fact that his plans were laid out long before I even existed.

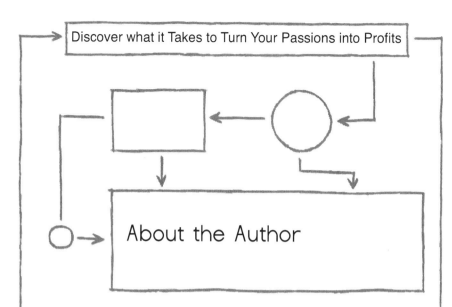

Discover what it Takes to Turn Your Passions into Profits

## About the Author

Justin Lukasavige is an author, speaker, coach, radio talk show host[1] and owner of Lukas Coaching, L.L.C. For more than 5 years Justin and his team have empowered people from all backgrounds to become debt-free, find or create work they love and work with *passion*! He's been called *America's Favorite Business and Success Expert* and truly has a passion for his work.

Justin created the Coach Training Program[2] because he felt a need to pass along to others what was given to him. His

---

1     www.pastdueradio.com
2     www.lukascoaching.com/coach_training.htm

passion of helping others improve their lives and businesses goes beyond his clients; he truly loves pouring his knowledge of business into other coaches so they can also grow their businesses. When coaching businesses are growing, people are being helped and their lives improved.

If you'd like a complimentary 30-minute coaching session with Justin to take your business to the next level you can make a request at LukasCoaching.com, or call (919) 342-0801.

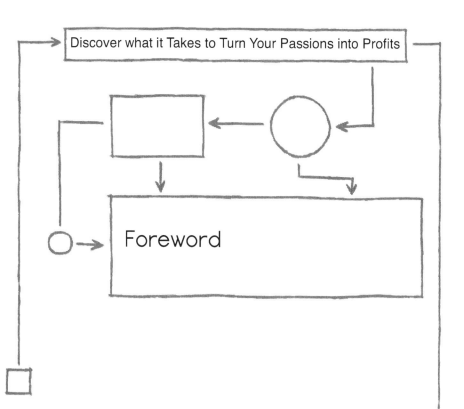

Discover what it Takes to Turn Your Passions into Profits

# Foreword

The explosion of coaching has been fueled by the continued workplace volatility, the downturn of traditional financial markets, the relentless stresses on relationships and the challenges of finding our purpose and calling. But can anyone be a "coach?" Justin Lukasavige confronts this hot topic at a time when it seems that thousands of people are simply presenting themselves as coaches.

In *Become a Coach*, Justin addresses the multiple aspects of successful coaching from both the coach and the client perspective. He draws on his own unique background and how that positioned him to begin the process of becoming a very successful coach. He covers the psychological components of coaching, the obvious need in the marketplace for coaching, and most importantly, the business side of coaching. Too many people have jumped into coaching having perhaps the personal attributes to coach, but lacking the business acumen to survive financially over the long haul. Having a coaching business requires more than empathy, compassion and understanding. It requires leveraging one's intellectual expertise and creating multiple streams of revenue that complement the one-on-one coaching process.

*Become a Coach* will help you set a solid foundation for bringing hope and encouragement to a waiting world. It will also help you thrive financially and to quickly rise to the top of this exciting new profession.

Dan Miller
*Author and Life Coach*

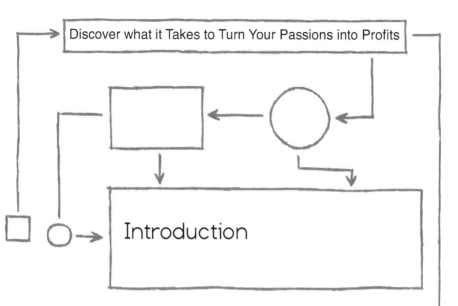

Discover what it Takes to Turn Your Passions into Profits

# Introduction

Welcome to the exciting world of coaching! Coaching is a process whereby you have the opportunity to use your wisdom and life experiences to help others improve their lives. As a professional coach, I have helped hundreds of families improve their finances, their standard of living and ultimately their lives. I have helped start businesses, improved existing businesses and moved people into living a life they were truly meant to live, all the while working with *passion*!

*My* passion is to help the people I interact with discover their unique gifts and abilities and then to help them develop an economic model which provides income for their families.

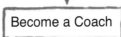
Unfortunately, I can only reach a limited number of people by working with them one-on-one.

I have discovered that by hosting a weekly radio show I can help many more people than I could ever hope to reach in my office. By simply tuning in, people can glean information from me without even having to leave their homes. You too can listen each week on AM 1030 in Raleigh-Durham, NC. You can also download the podcast and watch live streaming video of the show each week at PastDueRadio.com.

To spread my gifts even further I find a tremendous amount of joy in helping others become coaches and in turn pouring themselves into the lives of their clients. I live by Zig Ziglar's motto which is, *"You can have anything in life you want, if you just help enough other people get what they want."*

This motto has been a backbone of Lukas Coaching from the very beginning and I stand behind it today. My passion is to help others and I've found that as long as I am helping people improve their lives, I never have to worry about where my next check is going to come from. At Lukas Coaching we do not measure success by how much money we make, but rather how many lives we help change.

The purpose of this book is to answer some of the most common questions I receive from those interested in becoming a coach. It is not a definitive guide, but it should help you determine if becoming a coach is a good fit for you.

I love hearing from my readers, so if you have a question, comment or suggestion, please email me at justin@lukascoaching.com. I will do my best to help you move in the direction that combines your personality traits, skills and abilities with your values, dreams and passions.

If you'd like to read more of my story (or see the video) head over to lukascoaching.com and click on About Us.

*May you always work with passion!*

Justin Lukasavige

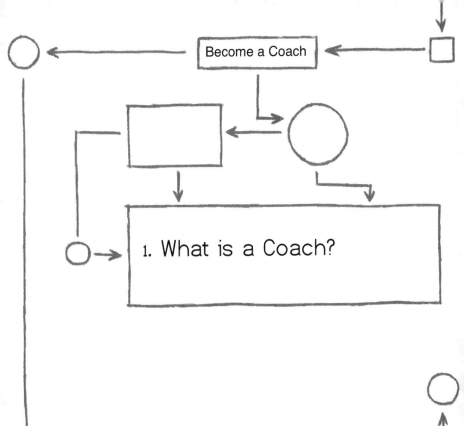

Become a Coach

# 1. What is a Coach?

When I first became a coach I thought coaches, counselors, mentors, and consultants were all the same. That couldn't be further from the truth. The differences are very important to understand; it affects how you help the people who need your help the most.

A counselor can most easily be described as someone who works to overcome problems of the past. The majority of counselors are certified and have degrees. Most states require this by law if you want to call yourself a counselor. A counselor usually holds a masters or doctorate degree in a field of counseling and has a high level of patience.

While it's a generality, I view counseling as not being very results driven. I don't want to downplay the importance of counseling; my team has referred a number of our clients to counselors over the years. I, for one, do not have the patience to be an effective counselor. Instead, I prefer to help my clients identify where they need to be in relation to where they are now. My goal as an effective coach is to do whatever it takes to help them get there.

A mentor can be viewed as a trusted friend or someone you look up to. I have many mentors in business *and* in my personal life. I'm very close to some but others don't even know I exist. In this case we look up to people from afar and model our actions after theirs. A two-way mentoring relationship is a great way for two or more people to spur each other toward greater levels of success.

A mentor can be your best friend and is probably the first person you call when you meet with victories or struggles, but a mentor does not usually work closely with you to help you define and reach your goals.

A consultant is the term that perhaps mostly resembles coaching. The word consultant comes from the Latin word *consultare* which means to discuss. Ironically, that's where we also get our word counsel.

It's been said that a consultant spends his time annoying workers while tirelessly striving to extend his contract. It's a hilarious definition but many people don't have a favorable view of consultants. In the loosest sense of the word, a consultant identifies problems, issues, or opportunities and usually ends there rather than helping a company or individual fix them.

Wikipedia (the ultimate source of knowledge) defines a coach[3] as someone who can direct, instruct and train a person or group of people, with the aim to achieve some goal or develop specific skills.

Essentially, a coach takes it to the next level and makes things happen.

Recently I met a counselor who had been working with clients for the past 20 years. She quickly voiced her frustration of being tired of holding her clients hands and stated that she's ready to see them move towards action.

If you want to see action from your clients perhaps coaching is the best fit for you. You must decide to become someone that can encourage, motivate and move your clients to the levels of success they desire.

---

3    http://en.wikipedia.org/wiki/Coaching

Discover what it Takes to Turn Your Passions into Profits

**Justin's recap:**
Counselor - Deals with problems of the past
Mentor - Someone to look up to
Consultant - Identifies problems
Coach - Results driven

25

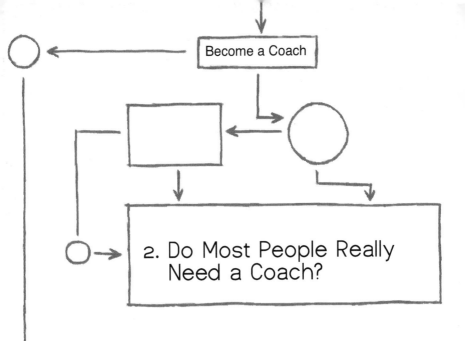

## 2. Do Most People Really Need a Coach?

Yes and No. Many people find themselves stuck in a rut. That rut may be related to their finances, their career or business or even their health. Whatever the rut may be, many people do not feel their life is going in the proper direction. I like the expression that a rut can be defined as a grave with the ends kicked out. To avoid getting stuck in my own rut, I have hired coaches, mentors and consultants for many of the areas I find I need some focus. I've also joined groups[4] along the way that support the vision I have for building a business that helps people.

---

4      Such as www.faatrial.com

Whether a rut truly does exist or if life is great, I believe there is always room for improvement in the lives of nearly everyone. Some of the most successful people on this planet have coaches, including Tiger Woods and almost every Olympic and professional athlete. Even the President has a board of advisors that help him think through the possible scenarios and develop the best possible solutions. Come to think of it, even Jesus surrounded himself with twelve disciples.

With that being said, I do *not* think having a coach is a good fit for everyone. I *do* think that everyone could use a coach, but a person's current mindset really determines if they will take the steps necessary to make a positive change in their own lives.

I meet with many people who are interested in having a coach, but sometimes it seems they only want a quick fix to their problems. If you remember the story of *"The Tortoise and the Hare"* from when you were a child you know that being slow and persistent over time is what really pays off in the long run.

As I mentioned earlier, my passion is helping others, but if I determine a prospect is not ready to take the steps needed to reach their goal, I will inform them that coaching is not going to be a good fit for them. It is really draining for me to pour myself into the lives of others only to have them not act and remain stuck in their current position.

Bad reviews of the service you offer always travel much faster and farther than good reviews. If a client chooses not to apply the information to his life, they may see your service as ineffective. I choose not to work with those looking for a quick fix for this very reason. I'd much rather spend my time and energy focusing on those clients willing to do whatever it takes to make change a permanent part of their lives.

So, while most people do need a coach, I believe there are those you are meant to serve and those you are not meant to serve. If you already have people coming to you for advice in their lives, that could be the best indicator you will ever have that becoming a coach is your calling.

Discover what it Takes to Turn Your Passions into Profits

**Justin's recap:**
Anyone who wants *results* needs a great coach.

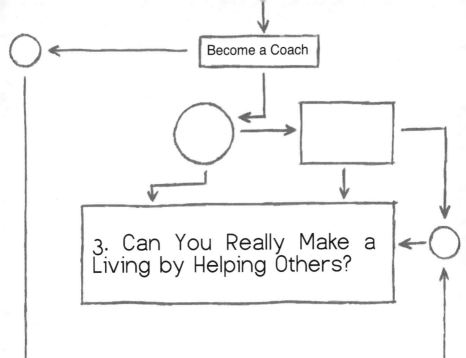

Become a Coach

## 3. Can You Really Make a Living by Helping Others?

Zig Ziglar's motto bears repeating here: *"You can have anything in life you want, if you just help enough other people get what they want."* I can't think of a better way to make a living than by using the gifts that God has given me to help others.

> *"God has given each of you a gift from his great variety of spiritual gifts. Use them well to serve one another."*

**- 1 Peter 4:10**

Be careful though; if you approach this with the wrong attitude it will come back to bite you. You need to help others because it is your passion and not simply a means to the pay raise you've been seeking. Helping others should be a part of who you are or you will never be a great (or even a good) coach. Jesus speaks many times to the Pharisees about this in the bible. In Luke 11:42, He rebukes them for giving out of the wrong spirit.

However, if you help as many people as you can out of the love of your heart, I guarantee your business will thrive!

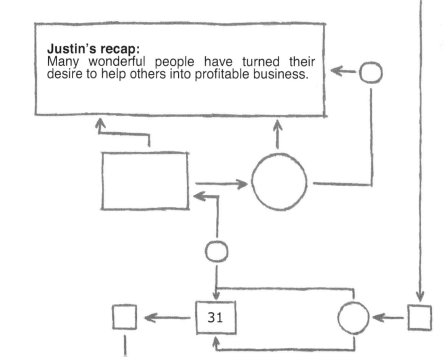

**Justin's recap:**
Many wonderful people have turned their desire to help others into profitable business.

31

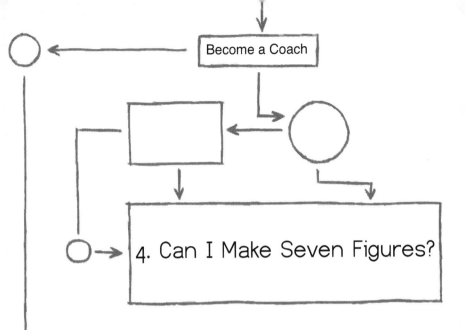

4. Can I Make Seven Figures?

I suppose you can make seven figures as a coach and there are coaches throughout the world doing it every year. Before moving on though, I feel the need to address something that will hold you back from making seven figures in any year of your life.

Between 1960 and 1980 Srully Blotnick, an American author, conducted a long term study[5] of graduate school students. In that 20 year period, he studied 1,500 people and grouped them into two categories.

5       Srully D. Blotnick, "Getting Rich Your Own Way", Jove Books, 1982

Category A people said they wanted to make money first so they could do what they really wanted to do later, after they had taken care of their financial concerns. Category B people pursued their true interests first, sure that money would eventually follow.

Of the 1,500 graduates in the survey, the Category A's, who wanted money now, comprised 83% or 1,245 graduates. Category B risk takers made up 17%, or 255 graduates.

After 20 years there were 101 millionaires in the group. One came from category A and 100 came from category B. I'm sure you've already heard the old adage that you must do something you truly love and the money will follow close behind. If money is the only reason you enter the field of coaching (or any profession for that matter), you're providing a big disservice to yourself and your clients.

Money should never be a reason to become a coach and if it influences your decision, you won't make the riches you set out to acquire.

Yes, there are coaches who make upwards of seven figures yearly. They'll surely be the first to tell you it took them years of hard work and perseverance to get to a level of greatness and profitability.

Become a Coach

So while you can make six or even seven figures as a coach, don't allow that to be the reason you become one.

**Justin's recap:**
Yes, but it's not about the money.

34

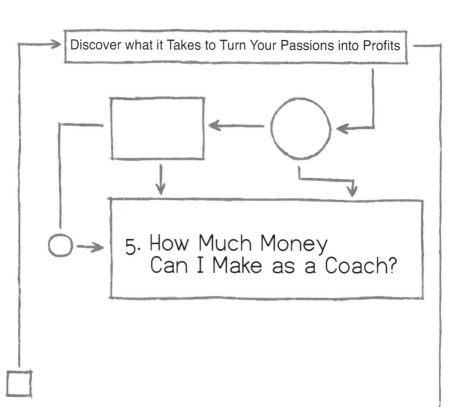

5. How Much Money Can I Make as a Coach?

This figure depends not on how much love you have for helping others, but on your ability to market your business and yourself. A recent survey of over 3,000[6] coaches revealed some very interesting perspectives on the field of coaching.

Of the 3,000 coaches who took part in the survey, 32% had been coaching less than 1 year. Another 34% had been coaching between 1 and 3 years. Only 12% had been coaching longer than 6 years.

---

6        Download a copy of the survey at
www.lukascoaching.com/sixfigurecoach.html

The respondents were asked how much money they earn annually. *A staggering 51% made less than $10,000 and another 12% made between $10,000 and $25,000!* Only 5% of respondents made more than $100,000 yearly in their coaching business.

This number amazes me. There are many people out there who need your help. If you're making $10,000 in your business it's awfully tough to provide help to those who need it. You're likely working another job to pay the bills when others need you most.

Please don't let these answers deter you from entering the field of coaching. If your passion is helping others and you have a gift for bringing out the best in your clients, then the sky truly is the limit in how much you can earn.

Let's take a closer look at these numbers. Sixty-six percent of those who responded for this survey have been coaching three years or less. In *"The e-Myth Revisited"*, author Michael Gerber points out that the majority of new businesses fail. As I look back on my business successes and failures, one thing that jumps out and even still glares at me was that early on in my business I didn't seek coaching from someone who had already been in my shoes.

I didn't seek expert guidance from professional coaches to help me grow my business until after my first year. I justified not hiring anyone because I was growing, albeit very slowly. *Boy was I missing out!*

When it finally seemed like I plateaued and had very little growth month-to-month, I hired my first coach. I spent an entire month's profit and traveled half way across the country to meet with that coach. Together we spent the next few days working with each other to take my coaching business to the next level.

It didn't take long for me to recoup my investment in the training and coaches that I hired. In fact, as a coach, if your personal clients put your suggestions in practice in their own lives, they should also recoup their investment with you in a short amount of time. That return on my investment was a very short *three months*.

As I write this, having been in business for many years, I still find myself hiring coaches. Recently I hired a sales coach to work with myself and my entire team. The bottom line is that if you're not growing, you're going the wrong way.

If you are truly serious about coaching full-time, striving to be in the top 10% of income earners (greater than $75,000 salary) is not out of your reach. It will take a tremendous amount of work to get there, but you reap what you sow.

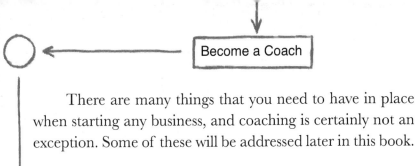

Become a Coach

There are many things that you need to have in place when starting any business, and coaching is certainly not an exception. Some of these will be addressed later in this book.

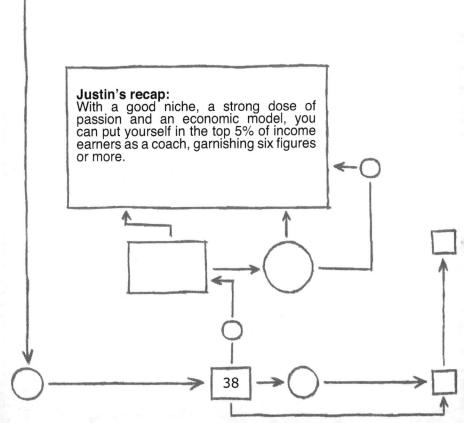

**Justin's recap:**
With a good niche, a strong dose of passion and an economic model, you can put yourself in the top 5% of income earners as a coach, garnishing six figures or more.

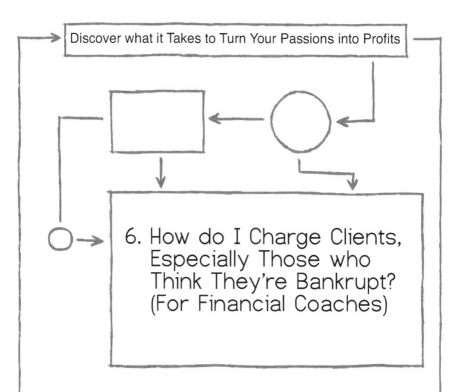

## 6. How do I Charge Clients, Especially Those who Think They're Bankrupt? (For Financial Coaches)

This is a great question, and until you can answer it, you will remain in the bottom 50% of income earners as a coach and may not last long in business. That's a shame because there are many people out there who need your help

My team offers six months of *unlimited* coaching to our financial clients. In the first 30 days of the program we schedule a minimum of four hours together and we pour a lot of time and energy into each client. Obviously there is a tremendous amount of value in our service, but unless we can show our clients how they can afford the coaching, we

are still dead in the water.

We have to not only show our clients how the coaching fee will cover itself over a 6-month period, but also how they will make money above and beyond what they pay for our services. Each client receives a game plan showing how the fee will pay for itself. We are always able to show clients how to reallocate their money so they can realize the full value of coaching.

For example, some clients are paying way too much for insurance. Simply replacing their current coverage with the proper type and amount will cover most of our fee. We refer many of our clients to a group of trusted partners[7] for these services.

This is what Michael Port refers to in *"Book Yourself Solid"* as an investable opportunity. It's a big phrase that means nothing more than this; your clients must get more value from your coaching than what they pay to work with you.

Think of it this way: Say you buy a pair of shoes for $20. On the way out of the store someone stops you and offers to pay $20 for the shoes you just bought. You'll most likely tell them no because you value those shoes at more than what you paid for them. We never trade money for something of

---

7       See www.lukascoaching.com/partners.htm

equal value. Instead, the products and services we buy hold much more value than the money we exchange.

Another way we help save clients money is by teaching them how to negotiate lower interest rates on their credit cards, or even how to negotiate settlements up to 70% off their balance! If a client has a balance of $1,200 on an outstanding credit card that hasn't been paid in over a year, my coaches can often negotiate a payoff amount of around $400. The $800 in savings easily pays for their coaching.

Sometimes clients just want their stress load reduced. Dan Miller, who is a popular life coach, currently charges about $4,500 for four coaching sessions. He could easily raise his rate because he has a vast waiting list and often refers out many of the clients who seek him out.

Dan is obviously not showing people how they can cover his fee by freeing up their income. Rather than a monetary return, his fee covers itself by reducing the stress involved with working in a job that is not a good fit. Along the way, most people increase their income as they move into the work they love, and that is exactly how we position our Career & Life Coaching services[8].

No one wants to be stuck doing something they hate for a living, and that could be a major reason why you are

---

8    See www.lukascoaching.com/career_life_coaching.htm

reading this book. You have to continuously ask yourself why a client would pay you for something they could do on their own. Are you saving them time or money? Are you helping them increase their income or lower their outgo? Are you saving them stress or improving their marriage? Will they lose weight and look good in a bathing suit this summer? Will their business profits increase to provide more income or time freedom?

These are the *benefits* you need to stress over the *features* of your service. Features provide a hook, but benefits provide a sale for you (feature) and food for your family (benefit).

Discover what it Takes to Turn Your Passions into Profits

**Justin's recap:**
Offer an investable opportunity. Provide more value than what your clients will pay to coach with you.

43

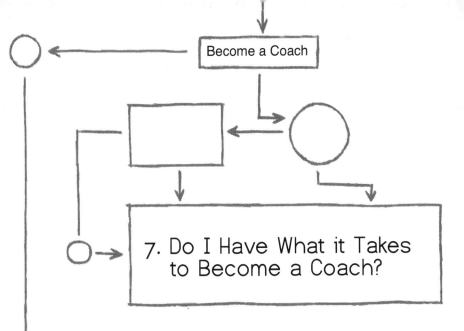

Become a Coach

## 7. Do I Have What it Takes to Become a Coach?

There is no training required to become a coach. If you have the life experience necessary to help someone through a stressful situation, that may be all you need to be successful. Check out *"How can Clients take me Seriously without a Degree or Certification?"*[9] for more on certification and degrees.

The 48 Days Coach page[10] displays a wide variety of coaches. Click on the 'members' section and you will see ADD/ADHD Coaches, Financial Coaches, Life Coaches, Goal Coaches, Health Coaches, Adoption Coaches, eBay

9        http://beyondpastdue.ning.com/profiles/blogs/how-can-clients-take-me

10       www.48days.net/page/48-days-coaching-connection

Coaches, Parenting Coaches, Marriage Coaches, Podcast Coaches, Technology Coaches, Music Business Coaches and Diabetes Coaches, just to name a few.

These people have valuable life experience which they can pass along to others through personal coaching, whatever their topic of expertise may be.

However, just having life experience is not enough to be an effective coach. Your personal tendencies foretell a lot about how you relate to other people, what kind of environments you are most comfortable in and how you think and communicate.

I use the DISC personality system with every Career & Life Coaching client that I meet with. This test measures your personal tendencies and produces a custom 32-page report all about you. Visit the personality profile page[11] to download a sample.

You *must* know your strengths as an individual so you can focus on them when working with others. DISC stands for Dominance, Influence, Steadiness and Compliance. Even if you think you understand where you land on each of these, you will be surprised, as I was, to learn that how you see yourself and how you behave can be quite different. You should never enter any profession or career field without

---

11    www.lukascoaching.com/DISC/disc.htm

first knowing who you are and the types of positions that are a good fit for your specific personality.

As I mentioned, there is not a single body governing the profession of coaching. You will find many coaches certified by one organization or another, but certification is not required if you know you have the passion for coaching and helping others. If this passion exists in you, your personality tendencies bend towards coaching as a vocation, and you have the life experience to back up your actions, then you may be able to help others improve their lives today.

Very few people ask me about my background and specifically, my training. If you are just starting out as a new coach, then certification and training may be more important to your clients. I have found that many clients want a coach with the experience and knowledge to help them through their problems. If you have a solid track record of helping others (clients, friends, family members, coworkers, etc.) your competency is more than proved.

With that said, I do encourage you to seek out training in your field. You should also consider ongoing training and learning as I do. You cannot expect (and neither should your clients) to know everything there is to know about your field, and you must always be learning as much as you can.

When I launched Lukas Coaching in 2006 I sought

the training of Dave Ramsey and his team in Nashville, TN. While the certification that I received certainly prepared me for working with clients, it was not a requirement for me to obtain before I began helping others. In fact, I had been informally coaching for three years prior to receiving that certification. Again, I had the life experience (my wife and I had worked our way out of debt), and my personal tendencies pointed toward coaching (I am a high 'I' and high 'C', meaning that I like people and details).

I have recently identified more than 300 programs that that will certify Life Coaches. These programs range from $15,000 six month courses all the way down to $40 take-an-online-test courses. In the latter you'll receive your certification in the mail within just a few days. The real issue here obviously is that certification does not equal competency, although it may help you with feeling confident.

Again, if people are coming to you for guidance in a certain part of their lives, this could be a great indication that you have what it takes to become a coach.

Become a Coach

**Justin's recap:**
Certification doesn't equal competence, but if you lack *confidence* in your ability to help others, take a few classes and read some books. Confidence will soon follow.

48

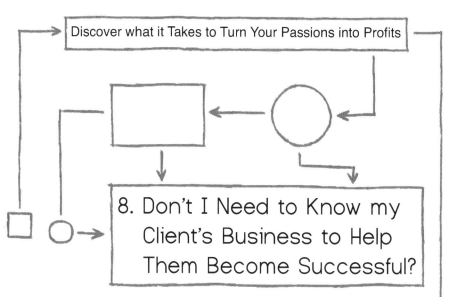

## 8. Don't I Need to Know my Client's Business to Help Them Become Successful?

A few pages ago you read that Tiger Woods has a coach. While Tiger's coach isn't as successful at playing the game of golf as Tiger is, he certainly is talented at helping others play the game better.

So, could you teach Tiger to play golf better? Probably not. But just because golf isn't your thing doesn't mean you can't help a player be more successful at what they already know.

My speciality is helping coaches build thriving businesses so more people can get the help they need. Recently, I helped

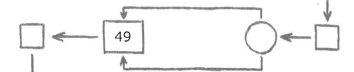

position a client to assist successful people (CEOs, board of director types, etc.) as they work through a divorce, separation or marriage problem. My client was perfectly positioned for this speciality because he's been through it himself and learned a lot about how to keep his life in tact while dealing with the emotions. He also has expertise in business.

My client positioned himself to be the only person companies will turn to when a high level worker who is vital to the company needs to be cared for.

Now, I don't know much about divorce. I've spoken to a few groups of divorced people and my parents have gone through it, but I'm very happily married to a wonderful woman. I do know what it takes to be successful in business as a coach and those strategies change very little with each possible coaching area. I can help a client build a Career Coaching business on Tuesday morning and be working with a Health & Wellness Coach Wednesday afternoon.

Notice that I have niched my services (also discussed in other areas of this book). I know a lot about becoming a coach and building a successful business. What you don't see me doing is working with clients in areas I am not competent in. For instance, I do not help people lose weight, although I can help those people set goals and become successful.

You don't need to know everything there is to know about the area you're helping your client in, but you do need to know how to help them reach their goals.

**Justin's recap:**
You need to know how to best help your clients reach their goals.

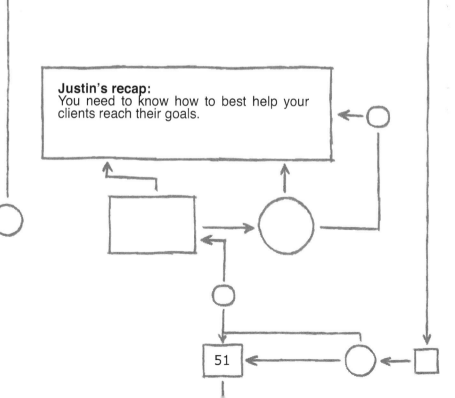

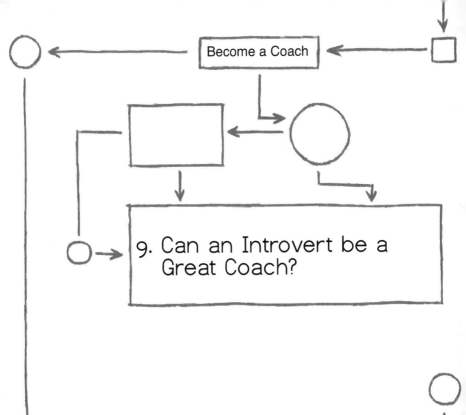

Become a Coach

## 9. Can an Introvert be a Great Coach?

Being an introvert or extrovert has nothing to do with being a great coach. On the DISC personality profile[12] I am an 'I' which stands for influencing. I's are generally social, outgoing, gregarious, life-of-the-party type people, but that doesn't really describe me. And yet I have hundreds of happy clients throughout the world who think I'm a great coach.

I prefer to work either one-on-one with my clients or in very small groups of people. I also like public speaking in front of large crowds, but I'm lost when it comes to large parties. I'd rather be in a small intimate setting with people I already know.

12     www.lukascoaching.com/DISC/disc.htm

Yes, you can be a great coach if you're an introvert, but how you market your business might be a little different from what an extrovert would do to market theirs. Introverts may hide behind their computers, not call prospects, and may not be good networkers. If going to a networking event with 20 or 200 people you don't know frightens you, then you'll need to find an approach that is a better fit for your personality - and believe me, there are plenty of strategies you can use to promote your business, including writing, having a great website and getting others to talk about what you do.

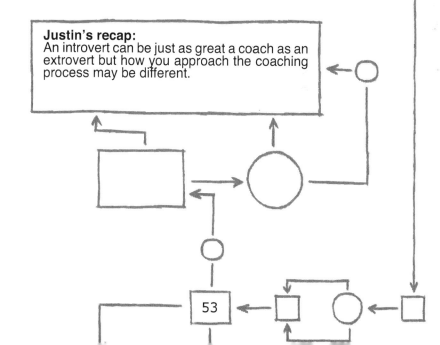

**Justin's recap:**
An introvert can be just as great a coach as an extrovert but how you approach the coaching process may be different.

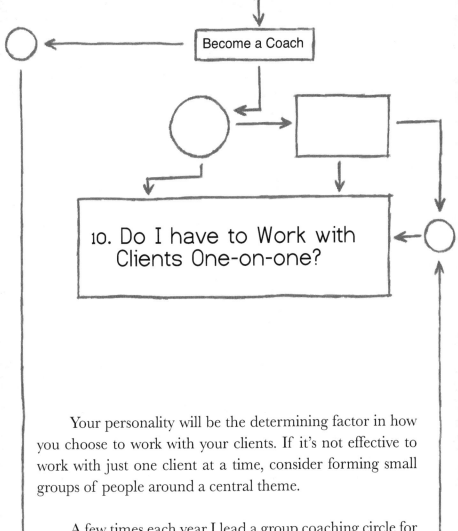

Become a Coach

## 10. Do I have to Work with Clients One-on-one?

Your personality will be the determining factor in how you choose to work with your clients. If it's not effective to work with just one client at a time, consider forming small groups of people around a central theme.

A few times each year I lead a group coaching circle for five to six career coaching clients. I use the 48 Days Seminar[13] as a guide, and many of the materials as well. I change the schedule to fit the group I'm working with and include many of my own materials to increase the value of the program. If you're a Career or Life Coach, the 48 Days Seminar is a great tool to get started working with groups. The material is

13    www.48days.com/products/seminarGroup.php

already prepared for you and you can add as little or as much to the class as you like.

Group coaching is usually more cost effective for your clients and more profitable for you. It's the best of both worlds. I tell people at times that I would pay more to be in a group when I'm learning. Instead of getting feedback and suggestions from just one person I get to lean on the entire group.

I've lead groups where I do very little talking. If you assemble the right group of people you'll end up facilitating instead of leading. Facilitating a group is more beneficial because it lends itself to the needs of the group rather than your agenda.

My team and I do group coaching whenever we can. Initial financial clients are offered a 1.5 hour group session to learn the basics at a discount. When we combine two to three families that need the same initial information it saves us a lot of time that we can use to grow our business and find more clients.

I already mentioned that I lead a group coaching circle based around the 48 Days Seminar for our Career Clients who desire to build a business. I also lead the Master Your Business program[14] for coaches and other service

---

14    www.masteryourbusiness.net

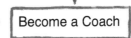
Become a Coach

professionals in a small group. When I lead this group I limit it to 20 businesses and teach it over the internet and telephone. It saves businesses the hassle and cost of going to a location and they can attend from anywhere in the world.

If one-on-one coaching isn't a good fit for you, think outside the box. There are many opportunities to help others that don't align with our normal thought process. Masteryoubusiness.net is an eight-week self-study programed designed to help you start your coaching business or take it to the next level.

Discover what it Takes to Turn Your Passions into Profits

**Justin's recap:**
Assess your personality to determine how you should best work with clients.

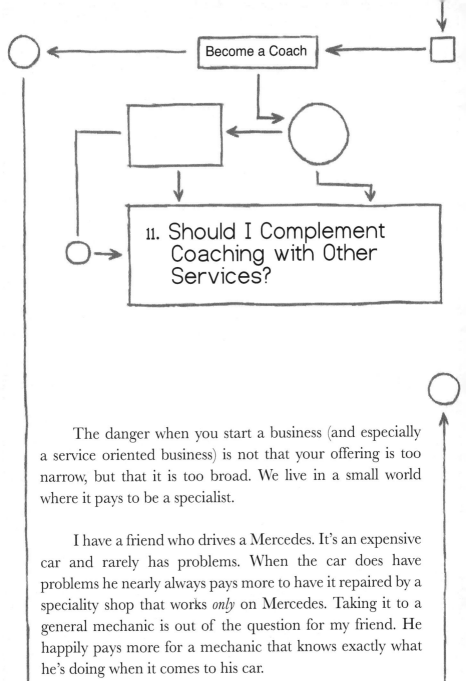

Become a Coach

## 11. Should I Complement Coaching with Other Services?

The danger when you start a business (and especially a service oriented business) is not that your offering is too narrow, but that it is too broad. We live in a small world where it pays to be a specialist.

I have a friend who drives a Mercedes. It's an expensive car and rarely has problems. When the car does have problems he nearly always pays more to have it repaired by a speciality shop that works *only* on Mercedes. Taking it to a general mechanic is out of the question for my friend. He happily pays more for a mechanic that knows exactly what he's doing when it comes to his car.

The same goes for coaching. I'm embarrassed to admit that when I began coaching I didn't just offer Financial Coaching. I also offered bookkeeping, website and graphic design and a whole host of other unrelated services. I actually had a church call me on it. They wanted to recommend me as a Financial Coach to their congregation, but they wondered what all the other stuff on my website was about. I stumbled around it and told them I wasn't offering it anymore (it had been a while since I had new customers in those areas--go figure) and I hadn't removed it from the website. Believe me, I pulled those services from the website quickly after that phone call.

When you can find a specialist anywhere in the world you tend not to work with a generalist, even though they may be in the same area as you.

> ***"You cannot make it as a wandering generality. You must become a meaningful specific."***
> **- Zig Ziglar**

I quickly dropped everything but Financial Coaching even though my income decreased slightly as I did so. It wasn't long before my market caught on though, and it quickly rebounded - and then some!

I built my business so rapidly that other businesses

were asking me how I did it. I couldn't take time away from paying financial clients to answer questions and help coaches and other business owners, so I decided to see if I could bring business coaching on as a service. It grew so rapidly that I had to bring on more Financial Coaches so I could focus 100% on businesses and coaches. I now have a Lead Financial Coach and I work with very few people in that area, choosing instead to focus my efforts on businesses and coaches.

If your market is telling you to offer something you don't currently offer, then it might be time to do it. Step back and evaluate your business and if it makes sense to branch out, then get started.

Don't ever confuse your primary offering with unrelated services. It wouldn't make sense to be a Career Coach and offer IT coaching, gutter repair or copywriting services for example. They are unrelated to each other and you'll have a hard time convincing your market of your expertise when it appears that you do so many unrelated things.

Discover what it Takes to Turn Your Passions into Profits

**Justin's recap:**
Make sure to visit lukascoaching.com/sixfigurecoach.html to download a free six-figure coaching model.

61

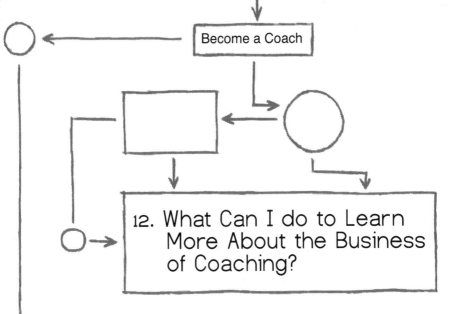

Become a Coach

12. What Can I do to Learn More About the Business of Coaching?

Read. I could stop there and that would be enough, but I'm committed to telling you all that I know. Dr. Thomas Stanley states in his definitive study of rich people ("The Millionaire Next Door") that the average millionaire reads at least one nonfiction book per month. If you want to coach America's next millionaire (and be one yourself) you need to be reading at least that many. I joke that I want to be a multimillionaire so I try to read at least two or three books each month.

You really can become an expert on any subject you wish if you just read three books on that subject. That's all it takes! If you want to be an expert and be good at coaching while maintaining a thriving coaching business, then you *need* to be reading.

If you don't know where to begin, just head to your library or local book store. Read the money section if you want to be a financial coach, the business section if you want to be a business coach, the career section if you want to be a career coach, or the health section if you want to be a weight-loss coach. If you are still stuck or are looking for more ideas, feel free to check out our suggested reading list[15]. You will find many great books listed there to get you up and running in no time.

On top of reading books, consider subscribing to magazines of interest to you and your clients. Expanding your knowledge beyond books is a good idea and you will have the opportunity to stay on top of the ever-changing world we live in.

Blogs are another great (and free!) way to learn. You can subscribe to most for free and receive an update any time a post is made. Check out our blog[16] to see an example. We have a list posted of other blogs and resources of interest.

Another great, and usually free, method of learning is

---

15      www.lukascoaching.com/reading.html
16      www.lukascoaching.com/blog

to subscribe to newsletters and other sources of information online. Our Reader's Group[17] email goes out weekly to a dedicated list of subscribers. They receive (for free) tips on money, business and career issues affecting our society today. You'll also see there are some great gifts that we give away with every subscription. Our members have told me they feel like they've hit the lottery because of all the great free information they receive.

Prior to starting Lukas Coaching I attended Small Business Administration (SBA) classes[18] at our local community college. These classes are generally free and cover topics such as taxes, business startup issues, marketing, networking, etc. The classes are a valuable resource to new or current business owners - and did I mention most of them are FREE?

I have attended many seminars and continue to do so to this day. I like to take friends and clients with me to big seminars as part of ongoing networking. They know that I care about helping them improve their businesses and that I value their friendship.

---

17    www.lukascoaching.com/joinus.html
18    www.sba.gov

*"Education makes people easy to lead, but difficult to drive; easy to govern, but impossible to enslave."*
**– Henry Peter Brougham**

One final thing I suggest you consider is going through coaching[19] yourself. Regardless of whether you have been operating for years or are brand new to coaching, having someone who will walk along side of you and help you through the up's and down's is invaluable.

I have had ongoing relationships with coaches across the country who have helped me improve my business and the services I offer to my clients. I don't think twice about paying $2,000 or more for a few days of coaching from a coach who can help me improve what I do. It has been my experience that by instituting the changes they recommend, I quickly recoup my investment. That is exactly what coaching should achieve.

---

19    www.lukascoaching.com/coach_training.htm

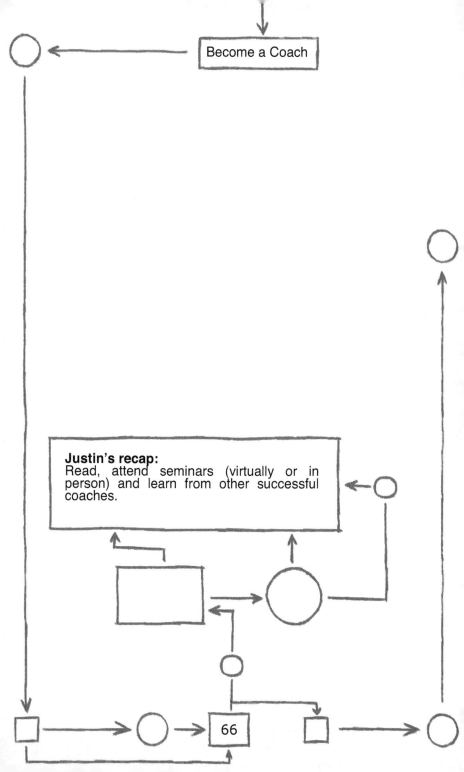

Become a Coach

**Justin's recap:**
Read, attend seminars (virtually or in person) and learn from other successful coaches.

66

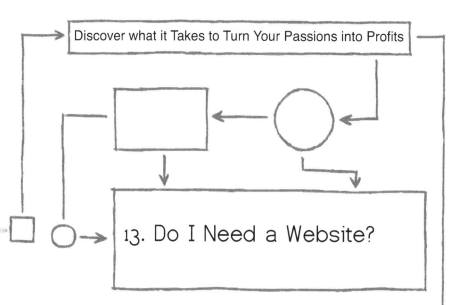

# 13. Do I Need a Website?

This is an emphatic *YES!* I don't mean to say you need a huge website packed full of resources, although it certainly would help, but at the very minimum you need an online resource that explains a little bit about you and your company, what you offer and how potential clients can contact you.

There are literally hundreds of things you can do with a website to improve your credibility, attract customers and create streams of income.

Your website can be as simple as Encompass Builders[20], which provides the minimum amount of information

20      www.encompassbuilders.com

necessary, or it can be packed full of information like I have at LukasCoaching.com. You need to have a quality website in place because in today's world, most people will want to check you out and do some research before meeting or even calling you.

How often do you see a general contractor with a website? There are not very many in existence, so the contractors who do have a website are automatically catapulted to the top of the pack if you're a homeowner looking for a project to be completed.

My first website looked like something out of the first Star Trek series but many people still gave me compliments on it. If you got past the horrible design issues, I did provide a lot of quality content which was not only beneficial to my clients but also to people that I have never even spoken to. Of course, if those same people took that information and passed it along to others, all the better! Viral marketing can be the best word of mouth advertising there is.

You do not need to spend a lot of money to get your website up and running. While there are many services that charge about $20 monthly to maintain your website, you can get one for much less. I spent just $4.95 monthly and an extra $30 per year for three domain names with the first website I signed up for.

I use 1&1[21] as my provider because I have found that they are tough to beat on price, service and all the features that I need. They aren't as well known in the United States but they are the biggest providers in the world when it comes to hosting and domain registration.

1&1 provides free web templates, which are included in the price, and they will get your website up and running very quickly. For basic information and a quick website, this is one way to go.

Other options include simply buying a domain name and using a blog. Inexpensive templates such as what MoonFruit[22] offers can be easy to set up, while Joomla[23] provides a completely open source application. All you have to pay for is the hosting service.

All of these resources will help you get your website up and running quickly. I cannot overemphasize the importance of having a very professional website for your business. If you have never designed a website or played around with one, now may not be the time to start. Find a professional[24] who can help create an identity for you quickly, efficiently and cost effectively.

---

21      www.1and1.com
22      www.moonfruit.com
23      www.joomla.org
24      www.moreprofittechnology.com

Become a Coach

When it comes to choosing a coach to help me improve my life, I won't contact someone with a poor looking website. It just doesn't portray professionalism and I'm looking for a professional. That is, of course, my personality and others may not share that view, but don't start out losing clients because they aren't impressed the first time they visit your website.

70

Discover what it Takes to Turn Your Passions into Profits

**Justin's recap:**
You need a website, but make sure it's professional.

71

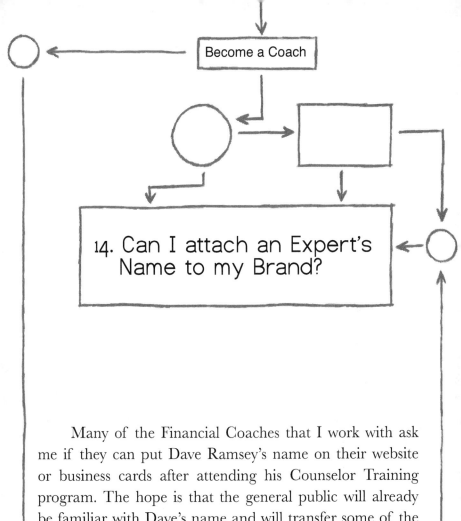

Become a Coach

## 14. Can I attach an Expert's Name to my Brand?

Many of the Financial Coaches that I work with ask me if they can put Dave Ramsey's name on their website or business cards after attending his Counselor Training program. The hope is that the general public will already be familiar with Dave's name and will transfer some of the credibility to them as a coach.

While you are certainly free to do this if you have been trained by Dave Ramsey's organization (Lampo Group, Inc.) or one of many other programs available, you must begin to pull away from simply being one of "Dave's Coaches." Your success and profitability depends on it.

The reasons are numerous, but you do not want to always be stuck under one person's umbrella. If you want to fill your business with more clients than you can handle you must establish yourself as an expert and not as someone just riding on another person's name.

Develop your unique brand - show your clients what is special about you. I do display my certifications on our website, but that is generally the only place you will see them listed. When I began my business, after having recently trained with Dave Ramsey and his team, I resisted the urge to market myself with his company. I wanted to sell my own services and products and not his company's.

I portrayed myself not as a Dave Ramsey Certified Financial Counselor, but simply as a Financial Coach. As a result, my business grew more slowly in the beginning than it could have, but I was able to break away from Dave Ramsey's shadow and become my own entity and expert in the field of finances. The idea is this: when people think about becoming debt-free I want them to think of my team of coaches at Lukas Coaching and not Dave Ramsey. When this started happening, I knew my mission was accomplished.

When a major news story happens in your town and within your speciality, reporters need *experts* who can comment on the story. If they visit your website will they find it plastered with other experts, or will it portray *you* as the

expert?

When the mortgage industry goes haywire and they visit your website, only to find all sorts of information on Dave Ramsey, they will most likely view him as the expert and seek out his comment rather than yours. This happens to be great marketing for Dave's organization, but does nothing to help you.

Until you establish yourself as an expert in your own mind, no one will ever view you as one. You need to develop top-of-mind positioning with your prospects and clients, meaning you should be the first one they think of when a problem arises.

Again, if you're lacking the confidence to prove your confidence, you may need a little bit of training. Find either a coach or formal training program to help you along the way.

Discover what it Takes to Turn Your Passions into Profits

**Justin's recap:**
Do it sparingly. You must become the expert.

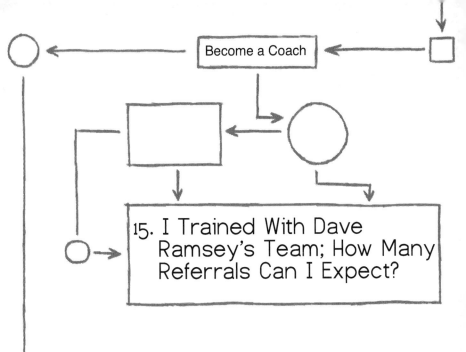

## 15. I Trained With Dave Ramsey's Team; How Many Referrals Can I Expect?

The answer depends on your market. If you are in one of the bigger markets such as Dallas or Kansas City, then you should expect many more each month than someone in a city that does not air the Dave Ramsey show. Dave's reach has grown tremendously with the addition of his evening cable television show.

When I began as a Financial Coach, the market in Raleigh, NC was not very large. Dave Ramsey's show was on a new, small, Christian station and the signal was not very powerful. I started out determined to create a name for *myself* and simply backed that up with the certification of Dave

Ramsey (someone that most of my clients had never heard of).

When I began, I received 100% of my referrals from Dave's website which was only 5-8 clients each month. I started out doing very little marketing, so initially I depended on people going to DaveRamsey.com to find me.

As my business grew, I did many things to make a name for myself, establish myself as an expert and bring in customers on my own. Recent website statistics show only 3% of visits to my website came from DaveRamsey.com in the past 30 days.

Generally, 47% of visitors to LukasCoaching.com come from referring websites, 32% of visitors come to the site directly by typing the name into their browser, and the remaining 21% find us via search engines.

Revisiting the previous question, no matter your market or which expert you are associated with, you do need to develop your own brand and seek customers through your own means of marketing. Additional referrals that come in on top of what you already do should be viewed as a bonus.

If I were to depend on referrals from Dave Ramsey, I would easily be in the bottom 50% of coaches making less than $10,000 per year. Don't get into coaching and think

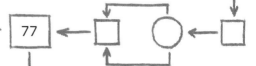

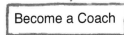
you can rely on any one source for referrals. There are many things I do to fill my schedule (more on that later) and any referrals from current and past clients, as well as partnerships with other sources, are simply icing on the cake. *I do not depend on them.*

The bottom line is that *you* are the expert. You can borrow some credibility, but build your business on your own name. The most successful Financial Coaches that I train are in very small markets and thus have to build their own brands.

Connect with a big name either through networking or training and ride that wave, but at the same time, establish your own business. This strategy is often overlooked but essential if you want to be successful as a coach.

Discover what it Takes to Turn Your Passions into Profits

**Justin's recap:**
It depends on your local market so be sure to build your own brand where you are the expert.

79

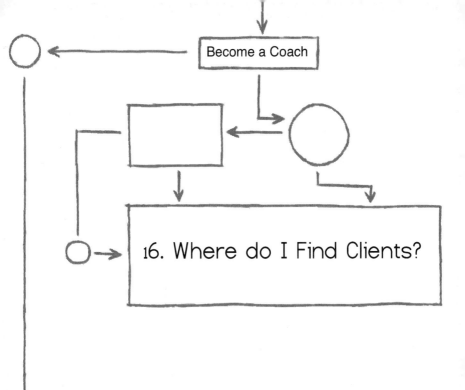

Become a Coach

## 16. Where do I Find Clients?

There is not one specific thing I can point to that drives clients to meet with my team. The following is an overview of some of the best strategies I used when I launched Lukas Coaching to make my phone ring with clients eager to meet with me.

Ultimately, you need to determine the best fit for your personality and implement a plan based around that to drive traffic back to your website and the services you offer.

## Speaking

Anytime you speak you have the opportunity to further establish yourself as an expert and fill your schedule with prospects and clients.

I have spoken in numerous venues for free, including special groups at churches and Sunday morning services. You can also speak at rotary clubs, civic organizations, government groups and other special groups.

I taught Financial Peace University[25] at no charge twice per year at our church for three years in a row. As a ministry I didn't make any money directly from leading the class. Teaching the course further established me as an expert and I began to meet with people who needed specific help after the class. Simply knowing that someone leads an ongoing class tends to strengthen credibility and can quickly position you as an expert.

I made it known that I was happy to talk, free of charge, with anyone during or after each class. Participants understood that if I met with them outside of class I was on my time and that coincides with a fee for coaching. Participants always understood and respected that. People are more than willing to pay for a service that adds value to their lives.

---

25      www.daveramsey.com/fpu

I created a Past Due: Boot Camp[26] that my team now leads in churches and businesses around the country. We lead preview events at no charge and the class is a very reasonable investment for a family to make. Speaking is an area that positions my team and I as experts, provides credibility and ultimately, paying clients.

## Writing

I write many articles every week. If you perform a Google search for Justin Lukasavige or Lukas Coaching you will find that almost 100% of the search results point back to our website. I do not get paid directly for about 99% of the writing I do, but it further establishes our company and me as leading experts in our field. Try searching even a vague term like "financial coaching" and see what you come up with.

It's important to point out that I have never paid for search engine listings or SEO (Search Engine Optimization). The writing that my team and I do catapults us to the top without much extra work.

## Host a Radio Show - Really!

I also host a radio show[27] each Saturday in Raleigh,

---

26      www.lukascoaching.com/bootcamp.html
27      www.pastdueradio.com

NC. This may seem like a big step, and I certainly wasn't thinking about it when I started my business; but as we have grown and met an increasing number of people, the doors just seemed to open. Anyone can do it.

Now you don't even need a traditional radio studio to have your own radio show, or even the cost associated with it. BlogTalkRadio[28] is a free website that allows anyone with a telephone to broadcast a radio show with very little knowledge of technology. Your account allows you to take up to five callers and even mix intro and outro music (music in the beginning and ending of your show) and commercials if you like. The only difference between that and traditional radio is people driving around in their cars won't hear you. Either way, the marketing of your show and getting listeners and callers is completely dependent on you doing the work to make it happen.

There are many things you can do with your specific marketing plan. Don't worry if you are not a speaker, writer or talk show host. You only need to find a handful of good marketing ideas and focus all of your energy on them. When you get really good at one strategy (and if you have time) bring another strategy into your business.

Regarding the Coaching Survey, 64% of coaches stated that referrals and word of mouth is how they generated

---

28    www.blogtalkradio.com/Lukas-Coaching

most of their business. Referrals and word of mouth are almost always the best and most cost effective way to fill your business, but do not let it be your only way.

While there are hundreds (and possibly thousands) of ways to promote your business, I focus on seven of the least expensive (mostly free) and easiest to incorporate into your business in the Master Your Business program[29]. I'll send you 101 Free or Low-cost Ideas to Grow a Business when you join our Reader's Group[30].

Even though I've narrowed it down to just seven strategies in the Master Your Business program, it's very important that you pick only one or two to focus all of your initial energy on when you're brand new in business as a coach. As you become successful in those areas you can start bringing others in just as I have done. If you bring too many on at once you'll quickly become overwhelmed and none of the strategies will work for you.

---

29      www.masteryourbusiness.net
30      www.lukascoaching.com/joinus.html

tough to get the time off to do that in a traditional job or if you have a storefront to maintain. That was not the kind of business I wanted for myself. My family and I are able to extend our vacations while I spend a few hours each day working with client's from wherever I am at the time.

Through the power of technology I can reach people in other parts of the country (and world) and even work remotely with them. Skype[31] is a wonderful free program that offers you the ability to connect with people around the world with a computer and internet connection. You can also add a webcam and feel like you're in the same room together if you like.

This isn't a technical manual on how to make remote technology work for you, but understand that options do exist that allow you to meet with people who don't live in your geographic area. I've worked with clients in nearly every state and in many other countries as well.

If you want to meet with people remotely you must first become an expert in your field. Your business success is completely dependent on marketing yourself as such. Start local and then broaden your marketing to become an expert in other geographic areas. That's how I became *America's Favorite Business and Success Expert.* Use your network and if you don't have one, then by all means, build a network of

---

31     www.skype.com

Become a Coach

people who can help you grow your business.

**Justin's recap:**
Small towns could mean big opportunities
for your business.

88

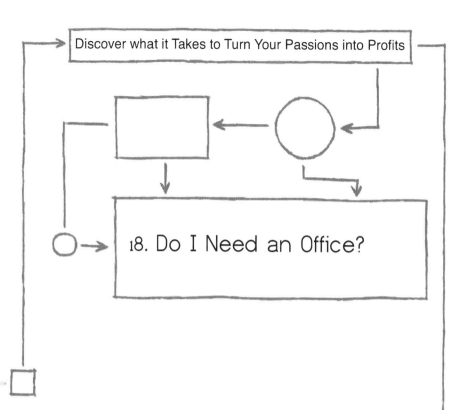

## 18. Do I Need an Office?

I launched Lukas Coaching in 2006 from my living room. Some days my work overflowed from that space and I had to move to the kitchen table. Our house is only three bedrooms and we had no spare room at the time, so if I needed a quiet place to talk on the phone I would often move my computer into our bedroom. There is nothing like working from the comfort of your own bed! I'm just kidding about that, it's actually horribly uncomfortable.

When I outgrew my home I met in an open office space at my church. All I had were three chairs, a desk, and a monitor that I brought each time to plug into my laptop.

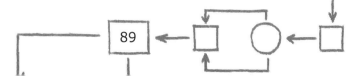

I was truly mobile. The church graciously agreed to let me try out my new business and believed wholeheartedly in what I was trying to accomplish. I didn't sign any agreement with them and operated simply on an understanding that I would clean up after myself. They could kick me out at any point. During that time I didn't even meet with anyone who attended our church. The church leadership loved exposing our community to the church and it was definitely a win for me.

I also needed to convince myself that this business was going to be financially viable before branching out and taking on the further expense of a monthly lease payment. It was not until November of 2006 that I signed the lease on my first office for $375 per month. A great resource in which to find spare rooms and small offices is Craigslist[32]. I have found two of my past offices there as well as an excellent agent who helped me find our current space.

Other ideas for office space include renting conference rooms, having an agreement with an office owner to utilize a room on an as-needed basis or even coaching directly over the phone. I coach with clients throughout the country (and all over the world) and rarely meet many of them in person. It fits my personality well and it may fit yours too.

I don't encourage you to meet with clients in their homes

---

32    www.craigslist.org

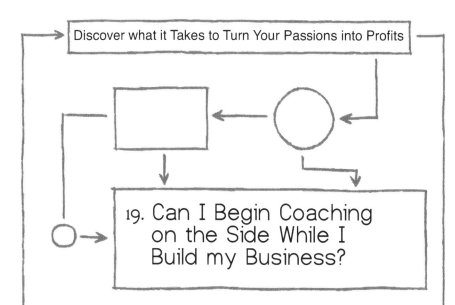

## 19. Can I Begin Coaching on the Side While I Build my Business?

I actually recommend that you do this. My background is varied and includes stints in management, company turnarounds, business ventures, teaching and most recently as an airline captain. Kids cannot be expected to pick the career they will work in the rest of their lives at 19 years old while in college and I was no exception to that rule. While I did not know it at the time, my background has set me up for working one-on-one with clients to help improve their lives.

I continued to fly for the airlines and operate Lukas Coaching until they both became too much and I had to make the switch. Believe me, it was a pretty scary transition,

especially since my wife wasn't working and I had two small children at home and one about to be born in a few weeks. During my time working both jobs, I barely had a full day off every week. It was a tough transition but a transition my wife, Christine, and I agreed was worth the sacrifice.

Many people think they don't have enough time in their schedule to start a business. With driving the kids around, working full time and caring for a family, where could you ever find the time? For starters, I haven't met anyone who couldn't spare four or five hours each week to change their lives around completely. If you turn your TV on, you are wasting some of the best time you have available.

You display passion for your business when you want to create a website or develop a new worksheet for your business rather than watching TV or the latest movie.

You can also try getting out of bed one hour earlier each day. If you can be productive during that time you will amazed at what you can accomplish. Many people may argue that to get up earlier, they would then have to go to sleep an hour earlier. Would that really be such a bad thing? You can spend five minutes online the following morning to find out who got kicked off the island if it's that important to you.

I stayed in many hotels when I flew for the airlines

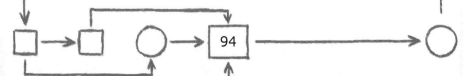

and there were many trips when I never even turned on the TV, even while spending 24 hours in the same room. While others were going out to party on a long layover, I was taking the necessary steps to move out of the work that did not align with my passion, into something that did.

There were other airline crew members who poured themselves into worthwhile ventures as well. I saw many pilots and flight attendants over the years obtain advanced degrees while flying and traveling at the same time. In fact, I wrote most of my first book "Keep the Change[34]" while on a very long layover in Washington, D.C.

*What could you be doing with your spare time[35]?*

It may be helpful to point out that I first developed a two year plan to build Lukas Coaching before making the switch to it full time. As I mentioned earlier, I first hired a coach for my business 12 months after starting up. Shortly thereafter I realized it was taking me way longer to build my business than it should. I was making money but spinning my wheels in certain areas and not growing my profits the way I should have been.

---

34      www.lukascoaching.com/keep_the_change.htm
35      http://bit.ly/34UgGX

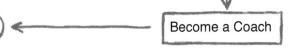

Become a Coach

I made the transition to a full time coach and business owner 20 months after starting Lukas Coaching; four months earlier than my original plan. I've helped many coaches do it in 12 months or less and I sincerely believe that time frame to be ideal.

Building a business takes a lot of time and energy. It's very hard on your family so the faster you put systems in place and become profitable, the better!

**Justin's recap:**
Not only is it an option to build your business on the side but it's also recommended to do so.

revenue should flow through your business each month. But don't stop there. It's great if $5,000, $10,000 or more comes in, but you need to know *where* it's coming from.

Here's an example. If your average client fee is $500 and you want to make $5,000 in revenues next month, then you need 10 clients. If you know your conversion ratio of prospects to clients is 50% then you need to meet with 20 prospects next month to close with 10 of them.

Let's take it just one step further. This is what I do with each of my Coach Training clients and it's imperative for the health of your business. You must plan the actions you'll take to make appointments with these 20 prospects. In fact, you'll most likely need 30 or more people to call or email to set those 20 appointments.

Now that you have realistic numbers you'll know exactly what you need to do to make the revenue and profits you went in business to make. At this rate, if you want to make $10,000 monthly (a six-figure income!), at an average of $500 per client, you'll need to have 60 or more prospects call or email to request a consultation with you.

There are also two other things you can do. You can increase your fees or you can make sure that only your ideal clients from your target market are contacting you. This all happens when you build a very solid foundation for your

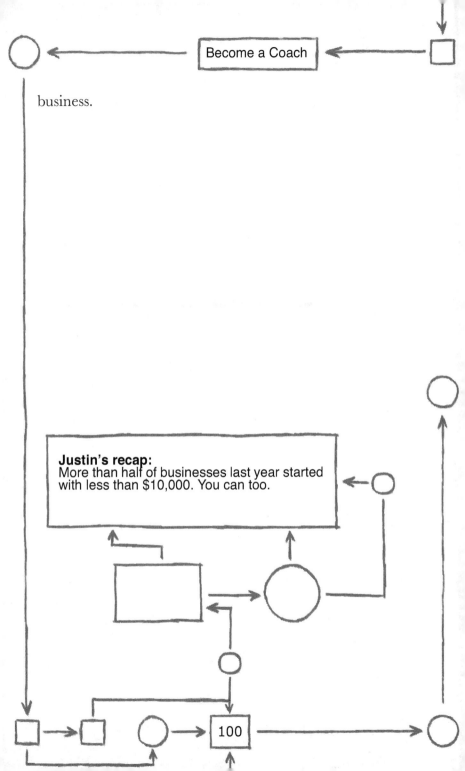

Become a Coach

business.

**Justin's recap:**
More than half of businesses last year started with less than $10,000. You can too.

100

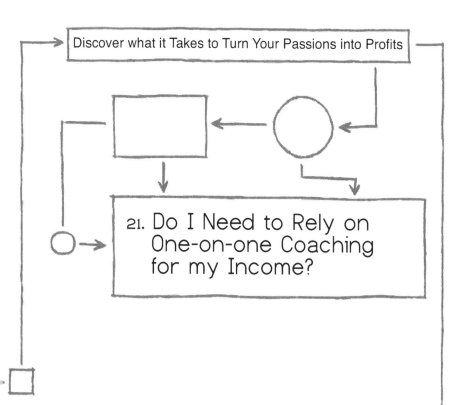

## 21. Do I Need to Rely on One-on-one Coaching for my Income?

While most new coaches (and some who have been coaching for many years) rely on coaching for 100% of their revenue I don't think it's a very good idea. Let's talk about risk.

If you're working in a traditional job right now all it takes is a decision by one person and you could be out of a job. When you're self-employed many clients simultaneously have to decide not to work with you before you're out of work. Similarly, if the only revenue stream your business has is when you work one-on-one with clients, you're leaving yourself open to risk.

Allow me to illustrate this point with a Venn Diagram. A Venn Diagram (as pictured here) is simply three overlapping circles. There are seven unique areas where you should begin to identify independent revenue streams in your business.

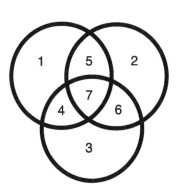

When you begin your business, coaching will likely be in the middle of your diagram (#7). We could also call this your sweet spot (as Max Lucado would call it), or where you shine and are most productive and profitable.

If you want to further remove risk in your business you need to branch out beyond trading your time for dollars. In the world of investing this is called diversification. No intelligent investor ties up all of his resources in only one area and neither should you in your business.

Keep in mind that your diagram can change over time.

Just because you begin with coaching in the middle does not mean it must remain there. You might have a passion for reaching people through speaking and thus focus the majority of your time getting paid to speak and perhaps even selling products at the same time.

The following are a few ideas to add multiple streams of revenue into your business:

- Coaching
- Speaking
- Writing (articles, books, magazines, etc.)
- Product sales (online or at events where you speak: books, workbooks, CDs, DVDs, info products and other products that compliment what you do
- Group coaching
- Radio show (monetize it by selling advertising space while promoting your business)
- Seminars and/or workshops
- Joint venture (partner with others to sell products or services; yours or theirs)
- Affiliate sales[36]
- Access to a membership site (continuity program)

. . . and the list goes on and on.

---

36    Getting paid to promote other's products or services

Set aside time to plan this out if you haven't. Most doctors, lawyers, CPAs, attorneys and dentists rely on linear income. That is, when they work they get paid. If they don't work directly with clients, they don't get paid.

If being tied to an office or getting paid only for the time you put in doesn't appeal to you, then you need to design residual income streams into your business. Residual means you do it once and get paid multiple times for the same work. An example would be writing a book and getting paid every time someone buys it.

If you spend 100 hours writing a book and sell it to 100 people at a profit of $10 each you'll earn $1,000 for your time, or $10 per hour. When you do the same work but increase your book sales to 5,000 people you'll earn $50,000 or $500 per hour.

This example doesn't take into account the time you spend marketing and selling the book, but you can see where I'm going. You *need* systems in place in your business that will allow you to break away from trading your time for money and that's what residual income is all about.

Discover what it Takes to Turn Your Passions into Profits

**Justin's recap:**
You need to design multiple streams of revenue, many of which should be residual instead of linear.

105

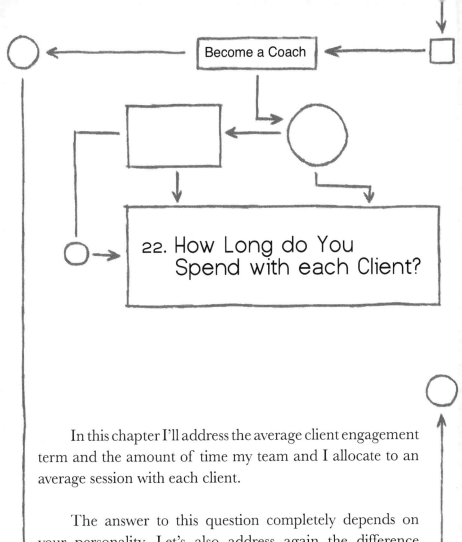

Become a Coach

## 22. How Long do You Spend with each Client?

In this chapter I'll address the average client engagement term and the amount of time my team and I allocate to an average session with each client.

The answer to this question completely depends on your personality. Let's also address again the difference between counseling and coaching.

Counseling relationships can sometimes last many years while coaching relationships (remember that coaching is results oriented) tend to last anywhere from a few weeks to a few months. In some instances I do work longer term with

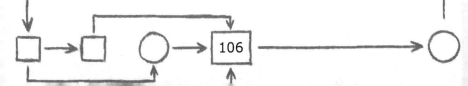

some of my business clients to help them start and/or grow their businesses.

Now for the personality part. I know coaches who prefer to spend no more than thirty to sixty minutes in each session with a client. This short amount of time doesn't allow me to go deep enough with my clients so I tend to spend about one-and-a-half to two hours each time we meet. This purely addresses my personality and there is nothing wrong with spending more or less time working with someone.

So here's how we do it.

## Financial Clients

I started my business as a Financial Coach and offered a thirty day program. I would teach my clients everything they needed to know in our first meeting and I would spend two-and-a-half hours each time. At the end of thirty days we would meet again for one hour to recap, review and answer any questions they would have.

While this fit my personality I quickly realized it wasn't a good fit for my clients. I sometimes overwhelmed them with information and thirty days wasn't enough time for them to use it and ask questions. I quickly transitioned to a six month program. I copied this strategy from other coaches who were already having success with it.

To this day, I don't try to reinvent the wheel. Many of our programs are created from scratch based on the needs of our market, but whenever I can, I look around me to find what's already working and then I try to figure out if I can duplicate it. This is a smart strategy that will serve you well in business.

When I extended my financial coaching to six months I was able to raise my fee, but I didn't have to raise it that much higher. While six months was a good selling point, many clients didn't require that much follow up. On average, after the first thirty days, I'd spend only two to three hours more working with a client (in person, through telephone or email). The pressure is removed from your clients to perform and deliver results and puts more pressure on you and your company if you offer support for a longer period of time. By standing behind your coaching in this way you'll likely see the number of clients signing up with you increase.

You can see the details of our financial coaching programs at lukascoaching.com/financial_coaching.htm.

## Life/Career Clients

I expanded the offering of Lukas Coaching about one and a half years after launching my business. My business grew so rapidly that others were asking me how I did it. I offered to teach them, but since it took time away from my financial clients I began charging the advice seekers.

I only added Life/Career Coaching and Business Coaching to my mix after Financial Coaching was already a success. You don't want your focus to be too broad, especially if some programs aren't working well for you.

Immediately, I realized that Life/Career and Business Coaching were going to be more profitable than Financial Coaching. Results can be quicker to achieve and clients are generally not at the bottom of their barrels.

Initially my Life/Career Coaching program was offered over a ten week period. I met with each client for one-and-a-half hours at a time, once, every two weeks.

This program was also extended to six months in length after thinking through options that would best help my clients succeed. The majority of time spent one-on-one with my clients still occurs during the first two months. The remaining four moths of the program offer unlimited email access to me as well as the opportunity to spend up to ninety minutes more together if the client desires. The details of my Life/Career Coaching program can be found at lukascoaching.com/career_life_coaching.htm.

Become a Coach

## Business Clients

Business Coaching takes place over a three month period and encompasses ten hours together with me. Similar to Life Coaching, Business Coaching also includes unlimited email support during the entire three month period. I also spend between one-and-a-half to two hours during each session, depending on the needs of the client.

One-and-a-half hours seems to fit my personality perfectly. It also seems to be a good fit for the clients I work with. If you enter the field of health coaching you might determine that meeting once per week for fifteen or thirty minutes at a time works best for you. The point is to discover what works best for you and your clients and design your unique programs around it.

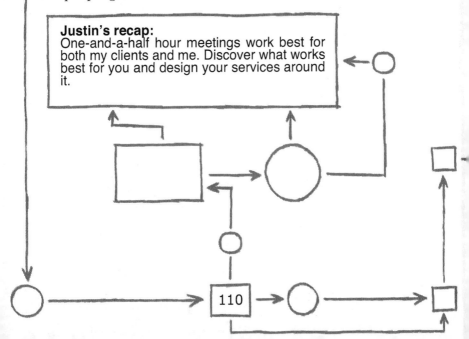

**Justin's recap:**
One-and-a-half hour meetings work best for both my clients and me. Discover what works best for you and design your services around it.

110

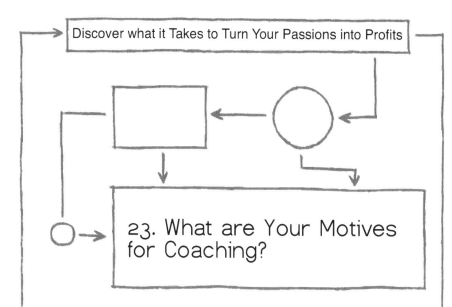

# 23. What are Your Motives for Coaching?

At least three things need to be in alignment if you want to do well as a coach. You must be sure you have the skill and ability to coach, your personal tendencies[37] are a fit for helping others and your values, dreams and passion align with the market you wish to serve.

I strongly caution those wanting to do something just for the money to rethink their plans. Common sense dictates you'll never be good at selling a product or service you don't believe in. If you have a tremendous dislike for credit cards, you will never make it as an agent selling processing machines to businesses. If real estate does not interest you

37    www.lukascoaching.com/DISC/disc.htm

but you heard there is a lot of money to be made selling homes, I guarantee you will only sell a few homes each year (if that).

The same is true for every profession. If you want to do well and prosper, you have to have a sincere passion for what you do. Without it you will barely eke out a living each month.

I didn't write this book because I thought it would sell thousands of copies. Rather, I wrote it because it combines my love for writing with my love for helping others improve their lives. The success of this book has already exceeded my expectations as I've gone through multiple revisions. Somewhere along the way I found I could make a living coaching others through their unique business situations and I'm loving it! When you use your God-given talents to help other people I know you will be blessed.

*"God has given each of you a gift from his great variety of spiritual gifts. Use them well to serve one another."*
**- 1 Peter 4:10**

Discover what it Takes to Turn Your Passions into Profits

**Justin's recap:**
Be confident in what you offer and your sales will skyrocket.

113

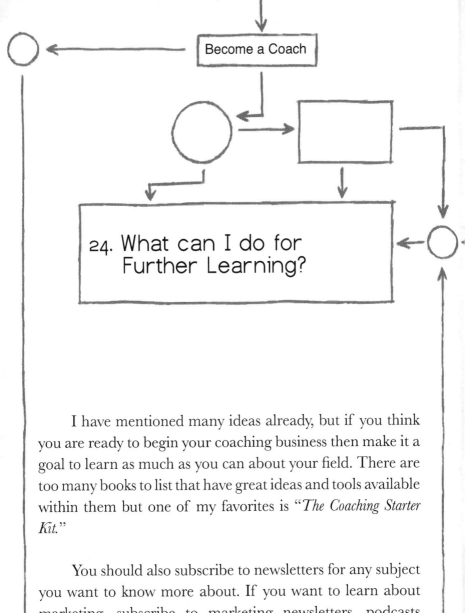

Become a Coach

## 24. What can I do for Further Learning?

I have mentioned many ideas already, but if you think you are ready to begin your coaching business then make it a goal to learn as much as you can about your field. There are too many books to list that have great ideas and tools available within them but one of my favorites is *"The Coaching Starter Kit."*

You should also subscribe to newsletters for any subject you want to know more about. If you want to learn about marketing, subscribe to marketing newsletters, podcasts and blogs[38]. You can subscribe to my Reader's Group at LukasCoaching.com/joinus.

---

38    www.sethgodin.com

Learn from other coaches and businesses. You can often do this for free just by observing their businesses from a distance, getting ideas from their websites and learning about what they are doing to connect their with customers.

Many business owners, and especially other coaches, are happy to spend time with you to improve your business or help you start it up. Too many people in our society have a scarcity mentality, whereby they do not want to share things with people for fear of competition. I don't. I have worked with other coaches in my area, as well as from all over the world to improve their business. That is just one more way I can use my knowledge more effectively to help the greatest number of people and I welcome the questions I get about coaching.

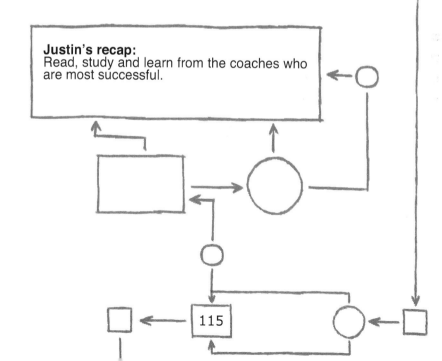

**Justin's recap:**
Read, study and learn from the coaches who are most successful.

115

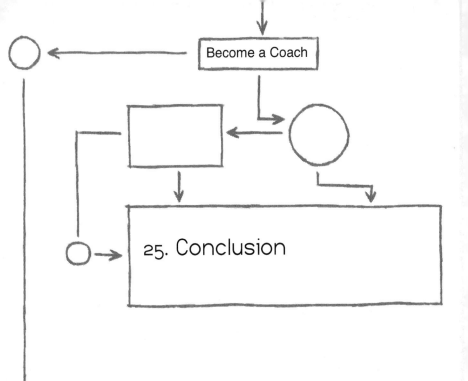

Become a Coach

## 25. Conclusion

 

I hope this book has opened your eyes to the wonderful opportunities available in the world of coaching. Helping others is a reward in life and an awesome responsibility as well.

Taking the time to first understand yourself is the most important step before beginning any venture, whether it is personal or business related. Once you determine your skills and abilities, your personal tendencies and your values, dreams and passion, you will begin to see and understand the ultimate plan that God has in store for you.

I learn more about myself and business every day and I learn mostly from working with my clients. I continue to make improvements in all areas of my life.

If you determine that coaching others is a good fit for you, then I encourage you to learn even more, develop a plan and then *ACT on it*! It is not until you begin taking your first steps that something begins to happen.

If you have questions as you develop and grow your coaching business, please let me know by sending an email to justin@lukascoaching.com. I would love to hear if this information has been helpful for you, and what I can do to help you build a business that impacts others.

I developed the Coach Training Program[39] to help you become as successful as I have, only at a much faster rate. For hands-on help starting or growing your coaching business, email me (justin@lukascoaching.com) or call (919) 342-0801.

To thank you for purchasing this book, I'd love to offer you a complimentary 30-minute coaching session[40]. Be sure to mention this book when we talk.

*Wishing you the best in your pursuit of changing lives!*

---

39      www.lukascoaching.com/coach_training.htm
40      www.lukascoaching.com/free_consultation.htm

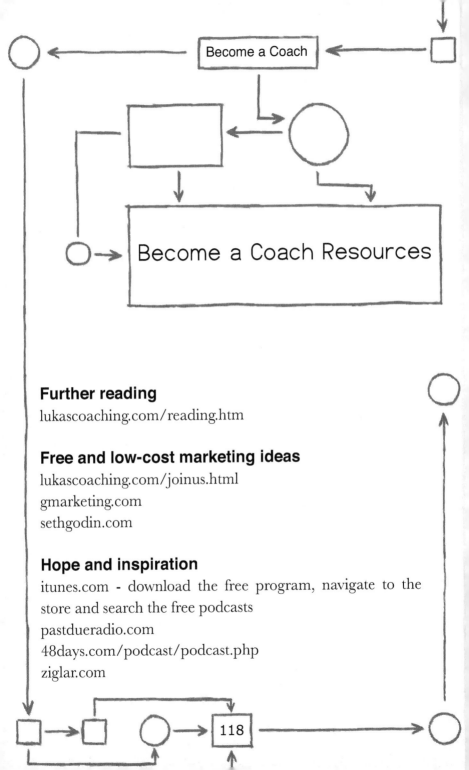

Become a Coach

Become a Coach Resources

**Further reading**
lukascoaching.com/reading.htm

**Free and low-cost marketing ideas**
lukascoaching.com/joinus.html
gmarketing.com
sethgodin.com

**Hope and inspiration**
itunes.com - download the free program, navigate to the store and search the free podcasts
pastdueradio.com
48days.com/podcast/podcast.php
ziglar.com

118

## Coaching resources

lukascoaching.com/coach_training.htm
certifiedcoach.org
coachfederation.org
coachville.com

## Resources I've used in business

lukascoaching.com/resources.htm#business

## Magazines

entrepreneur.com
success.com

Join the community at beyondpastdue.com. You'll connect with others starting businesses, getting out of debt and doing their part to help others.

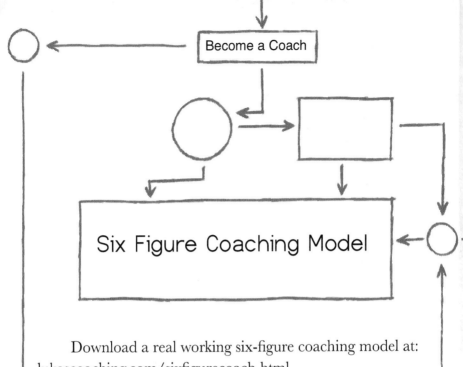

Become a Coach

Six Figure Coaching Model

Download a real working six-figure coaching model at: lukascoaching.com/sixfigurecoach.html.

If you have what it takes, it is possible to turn your passion of helping others into a six-figure business. As a coach you can use your gifts every day and be a top income earner in your field.

You don't have to work 80 hours per week and do things you don't enjoy; that's not what it's about. Instead, you need to work smarter so you're at your best when working with your clients.

Download a copy of the six-figure coaching model at lukascoaching.com/sixfigurecoach.html.

120

36173996R00073

Made in the USA
Middletown, DE
25 October 2016